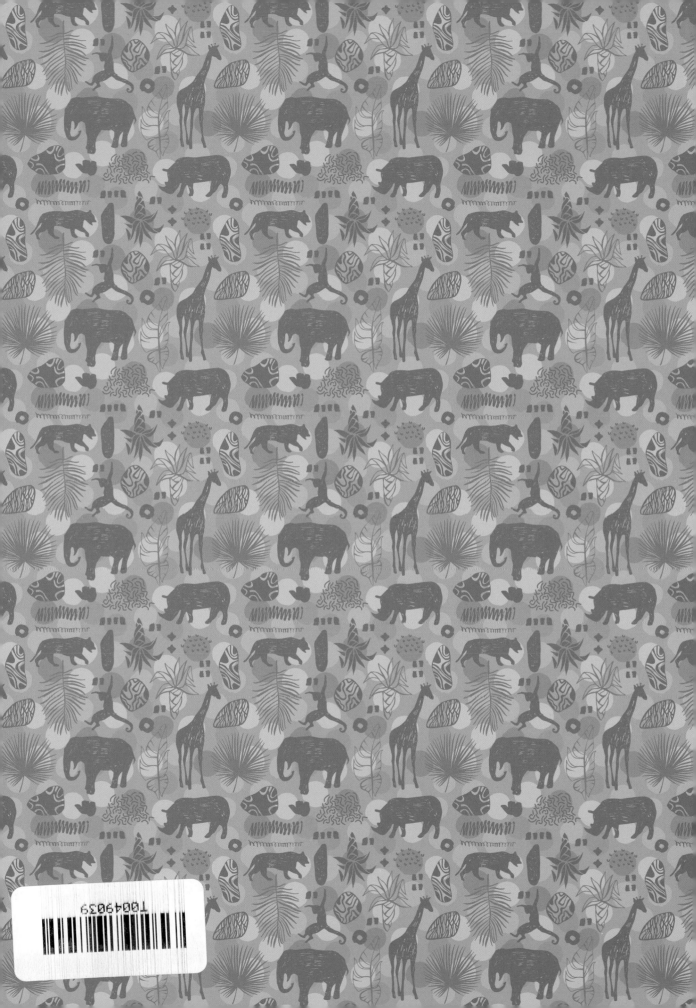

KIDS ASK ABOUT

SAFARI BABIES

WHAT do baby zebras look like?

WHO takes care of baby giraffes?

HOW do elephants grow up?

Written by Lisa McClatchy
Illustrated by Cindy Kiernicki

sequoia™
kids media

Visit us at
SequoiaKidsMedia.com
for bonus
downloadable content

Photography © Shutterstock 2022 AdaCo; Artush; BearFotos; Petr Bonek;
Mike John Brown; Coffeemill; Katja Forster; Lukiyanova Natalia frenta; Hein Myers Photography;
imageBROKER.com; Eric Isselee; Kletr; Joe McDonald; Dave Montreuil; Alastair Munro;
COLOMBO NICOLA; skorobogatova; slowmotiongli; calden Smith; phatthanasan suporn; tratong; ylq

Published by Sequoia Kids Media,
an imprint of Sequoia Publishing & Media, LLC

Sequoia Publishing & Media, LLC,
a division of Phoenix International Publications, Inc.

8501 West Higgins Road, Chicago, Illinois 60631
34 Seymour Street, London W1H 7JE
Heimhuder Straße 81, 20148 Hamburg

© 2023 Sequoia Publishing & Media, LLC
First Published © 2023 Twin Sisters IP, LLC. All rights reserved.

Customer Service: CS@SequoiaKidsBooks.com

Sequoia Kids Media and associated logo are trademarks and/or registered trademarks of
Sequoia Publishing & Media, LLC.

Active Minds is a registered trademark of Phoenix International Publications, Inc.
and is used with permission.

www.SequoiaKidsMedia.com

Library of Congress Control Number: 2022920275

ISBN: 979-8-7654-0176-7

KIDS ASK ABOUT

SAFARI BABIES

TABLE OF CONTENTS

LIONS

WHO are safari animals?

A safari is a journey commonly involving observing animals in their natural habitats, particularly in Africa. We call the animals that live in these habitats safari animals! Many safari animals live on the African savanna. A savanna is a tropical grassland.

SAFARI FACTS: LIONS

- Name of young: cub
- Gestation: 105-113 days
- Number of babies: 2-4
- Full grown by: 3-4 years

HOW do lions grow up?

Newborn lion cubs are helpless at birth! Their eyes are closed the first few days, and they don't have any teeth until they are three weeks old. Baby lions don't look like their parents. Their thick, wooly hair is covered with spots. Lion cubs weigh two pounds (0.91 kilogram) at birth and grow very quickly. When they are about three months old, they begin to eat meat.

ZEBRAS

HOW do zebras recognize each other?

The first thing baby zebras, called foals, learn after birth is their mothers' stripe patterns. This is how zebras recognize each other.

SAFARI FACTS: ZEBRAS

- Name of young: foal
- Gestation: 10-12 months
- Number of babies: 1
- Full grown by: 2-5 years

WHAT do zebra foals eat?

Foals drink their mothers' milk for the first three months and then begin eating grass.

WHAT do baby zebras look like?

Newborn foals have short bodies, long legs, and a furry coat. They weigh about 65 pounds (29.5 kg)—as much as a seven-year-old human! After foals are born, they take their first steps within an hour.

MEERKATS

SAFARI FACTS: MEERKATS
- Name of young: pup
- Gestation: 11 weeks
- Number of babies: 2-5
- Full grown by: 1 year

WHAT are meerkats like when they're born?

When born, baby meerkats' eyes and ears are closed and they have only a tiny bit of fur. Meerkats are usually born in a litter with 2–5 other pups.

WHEN do baby meerkats come above ground?

When they are four weeks old, they emerge from their home, a hole in the ground called a burrow. The pups will stay close to home for the first few months, under the watchful eye of their mother or another meerkat babysitter.

WARTHOGS

WHO are warthogs?

Warthogs are wild pigs. Warthog babies are called piglets and are born without any hair. They stay with their mothers in their burrows for the first 6–7 weeks. At just two months of age, piglets are able to follow their mothers everywhere they go.

SAFARI FACTS: WARTHOGS
- Name of young: piglet
- Gestation: 170-175 days
- Number of babies: 1-6
- Full grown by: 1-2 years

ELEPHANTS

HOW do elephants grow up?

Baby elephants are called calves and weigh 200 pounds (90 kg) when born. Baby elephants walk within one hour after birth, and within days they can move with the herd. Calves drink their mothers' milk for two years, though they begin eating solid food at six months of age. The entire elephant herd is involved in raising the calves, and grandmothers often babysit, just like ours!

SAFARI FACTS: ELEPHANTS
- Name of young: calf
- Gestation: 2 years
- Number of babies: 1
- Full grown by: 20 years

DID YOU KNOW?
Elephants give birth once every five years and each pregnancy lasts two whole years!

HIPPOPOTAMUSES

HOW are baby hippos born?

Hippos love the water! Mothers give birth in the water to a single calf each year. The babies, who weigh 50–100 pounds (22.7–45.4 kg), surface right away to take their first breath! The calves stay close to their moms, often riding on their backs when they are in the water.

DID YOU KNOW?

Baby hippos can drink their mothers' milk underwater or on dry land.

SAFARI FACTS: HIPPOS

- Name of young: calf
- Gestation: 227–240 days
- Number of babies: 1
- Full grown by: 7 years

OSTRICHES

SAFARI FACTS: OSTRICHES
- Name of young: chick
- Gestation: 5-6 weeks
- Number of babies: 7-10
- Full grown by: 3-4 years

HOW are baby ostriches born?

Three to five mother ostriches share a nest when laying their eggs. Mothers sit on their own eggs during the day, and then the fathers take their turn at night. Each ostrich egg is six inches (15.2 centimeters) long and weighs about three pounds (1.4 kg)!

WHO takes care of ostrich chicks?

Once the eggs hatch, it is the fathers who care for the chicks. It's not unusual for fathers to have as many as 15–20 fluffy chicks with them!

GAZELLES

SAFARI FACTS: GAZELLES

- Name of young: calf or fawn
- Gestation: 6 months
- Number of babies: 1-2
- Full grown by: 18 months

WHAT happens when baby gazelles are born?

When baby gazelles are born, their mothers clean them carefully! Once calves can stand and nurse, mothers pick a hiding place for them to spend the first two weeks. Mother gazelles return to this spot often each day to feed their babies. When calves are one month old, they start eating grass.

CHEETAHS

- Name of young: cub
- Gestation: 90-95 days
- Number of babies: 2-4
- Full grown by: 1-2 years

HOW do cheetahs grow up?

Baby cheetahs spend their first two weeks of life with their eyes closed. They are completely dependent on their mothers. By the time cubs are six weeks old, they follow their mothers everywhere.

WHAT do cheetah cubs look like?

Cheetah cubs are born with long gray-blue coats that quickly lighten and develop spots. By four months cubs are a tawny yellow and almost completely spotted!

RHINOCEROSES

WHAT do baby rhinos eat?

Within hours of birth, rhinoceros calves can walk and drink their mothers' milk. The babies begin to eat grass at three weeks of age.

- Name of young: calf
- Gestation: 15-18 months
- Number of babies: 1
- Full grown by: 6-7 years

DID YOU KNOW?

Baby rhinos are born without horns. They have a patch of thick skin on their nose, and in a few months, their horns start to appear.

BABOONS

WHERE are baboon babies raised?

Baboons live in trees and on cliffs, and this is where the babies are raised. For the first month, mothers will carry their babies in front of them as they travel. By the time the babies are five to six weeks old, they begin riding on their mothers' backs. Within months, baby baboons are able to sit up on their mothers' backs, just like a jockey rides a racehorse!

WILDEBEESTS

WHERE are wildebeest babies born?

Wildebeest mothers give birth to a single calf right in the middle of the herd! The majority of wildebeest babies are born during February and March. Calves can stand and run a few minutes after birth, and within days they can run fast enough to keep up with the adults. Calves eat grass within 10 days, but also drink milk for at least four months.

SAFARI FACTS: WILDEBEESTS
- Name of young: calf
- Gestation: 8 months
- Number of babies: 1
- Full grown by: 2-4 years

GIRAFFES

HOW are baby giraffes born?

Giraffes give birth while standing up, and the babies fall at least five feet (1.5 meters) when born! But this doesn't bother or injure the calves, who are six feet (1.8 m) tall and on their feet in less than an hour.

SAFARI FACTS: GIRAFFES
- Name of young: calf
- Gestation: 14-15 months
- Number of babies: 1
- Full grown by: 4 years

WHO takes care of baby giraffes?

Both mother and father giraffes care for their babies while they grow. Calves cannot run very fast at first and stay close to their parents for their first year.

SAFARI BABIES ARE AMAZING!

And humans can help protect them against threats like poachers and climate change. These animals can be found mainly in Africa. Most African countries have created national parks to preserve wildlife and wild places. The Serengeti National Park is filled with the animals featured in this book and is the size of Connecticut! Many local zoos also have exhibits where you can learn more about your favorite safari babies.